E S T A T E   P U B L ⸻ ⸻ O N S

CREWE

NANTWICH · SANDBACH

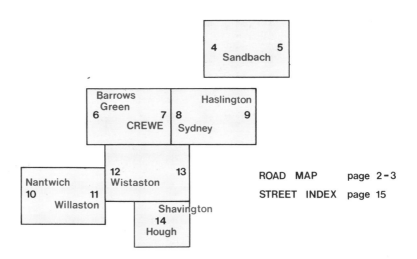

4	5
Sandbach	

Barrows Green
6   7 | 8   Haslington   9
CREWE | Sydney

12   13
Nantwich   Wistaston
10   11
Willaston
Shavington
14
Hough

ROAD   MAP   page 2–3

STREET   INDEX   page 15

Every effort has been made to verify the accuracy of information in this book but the publishers cannot accept responsibility for expense or loss caused by an error or omission. Information that will be of assistance to the user of the maps will be welcomed.

The representation on these maps of a road, track or path is no evidence of the existence of a right of way.

Car Park	P
Public Convenience	C
Place of Worship	+
One-way Street	→
Pedestrianized	▨
Post Office	●

Scale of street plans 4 inches to 1 mile
Unless otherwise stated

Street plans prepared and published by ESTATE PUBLICATIONS, Bridewell House, TENTERDEN, KENT. The Publishers acknowledge the co-operation of the local authorities of towns represented in this atlas.

Ordnance Survey® This product includes mapping data licensed from Ordnance Survey® with the permission of the Controller of Her Majesty's Stationery Office.

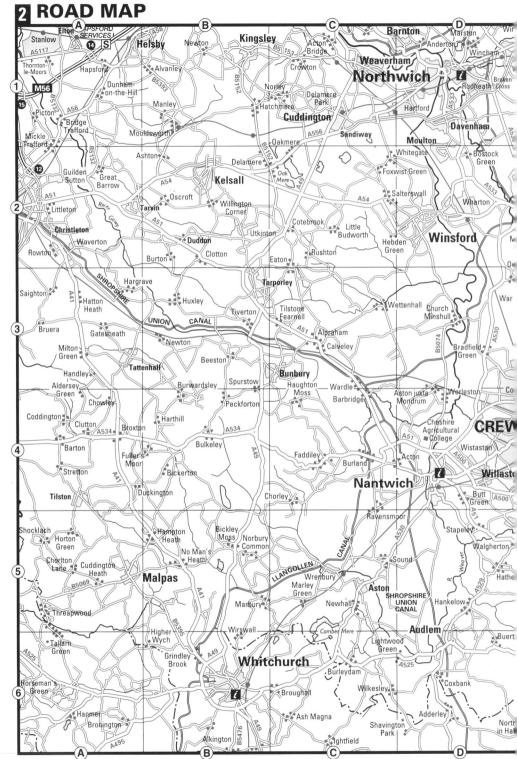

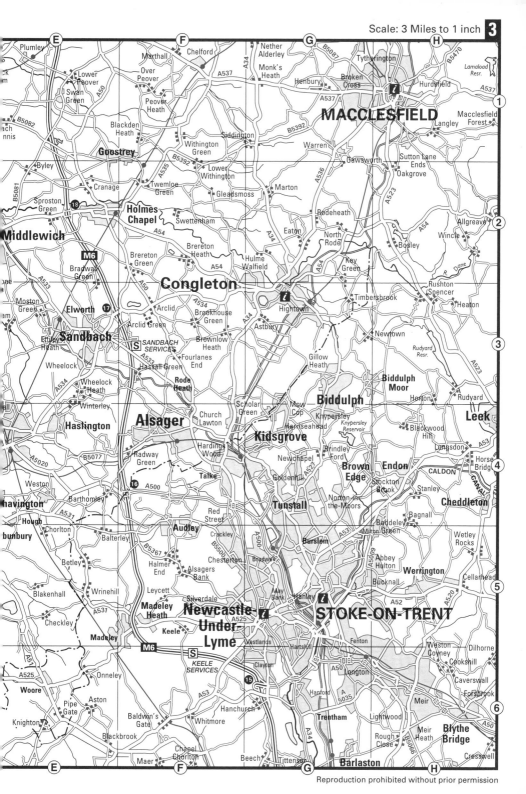

MACCLESFIELD

Middlewich

Goostrey

Holmes Chapel

Congleton

Sandbach

Alsager

Haslington

Biddulph

Kidsgrove

Leek

Brown Edge

Endon

Cheddleton

Tunstall

Burslem

Werrington

STOKE-ON-TRENT

Newcastle-Under-Lyme

Madeley

Woore

Blythe Bridge

Barlaston

Trentham

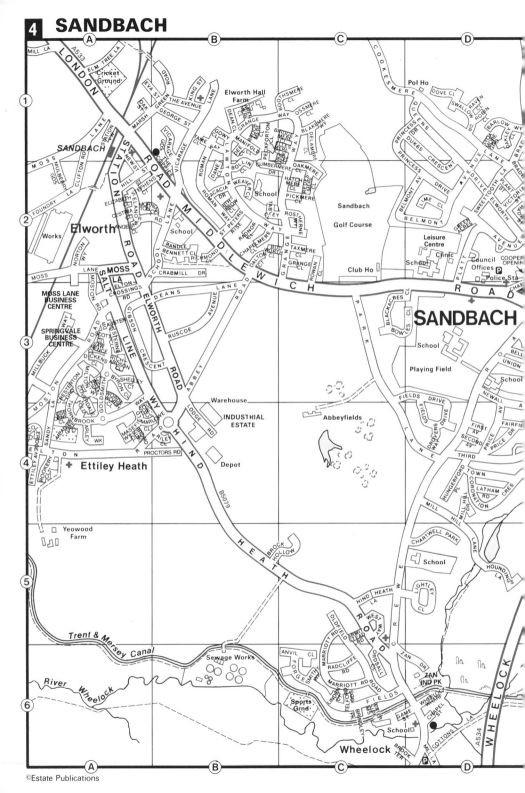

4 SANDBACH

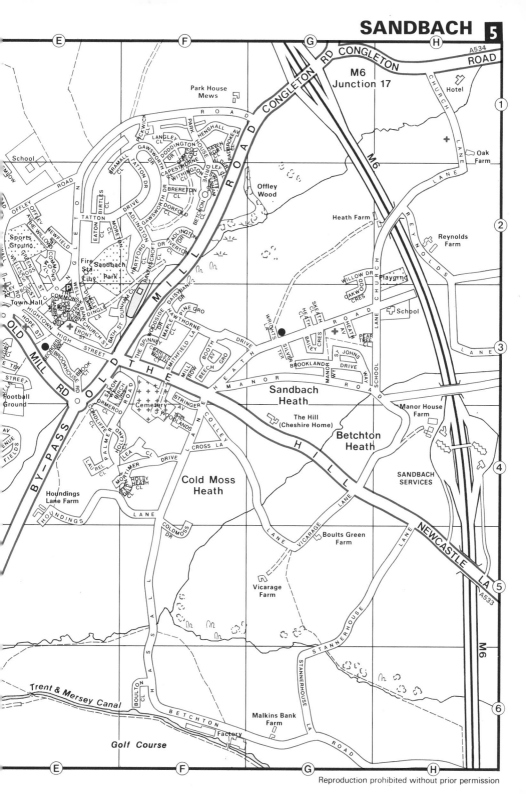

SANDBACH

5

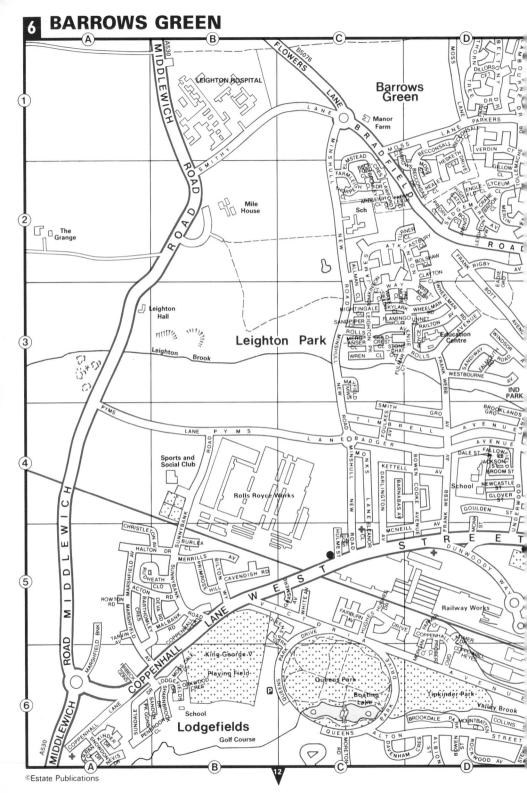

Barrows Green

LEIGHTON HOSPITAL

Manor Farm

Mile House

The Grange

Leighton Hall

Leighton Park

Leighton Brook

Sports and Social Club

Rolls Royce Works

Education Centre

IND PARK

School

Railway Works

King George V Playing Field

Queens Park

Boating Lake

Tipkinder Park

Valley Brook

Lodgefields

Golf Course

School

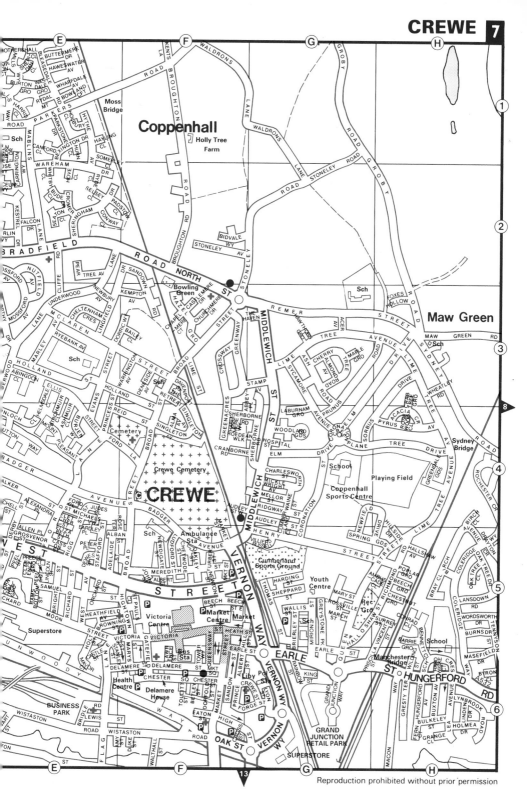

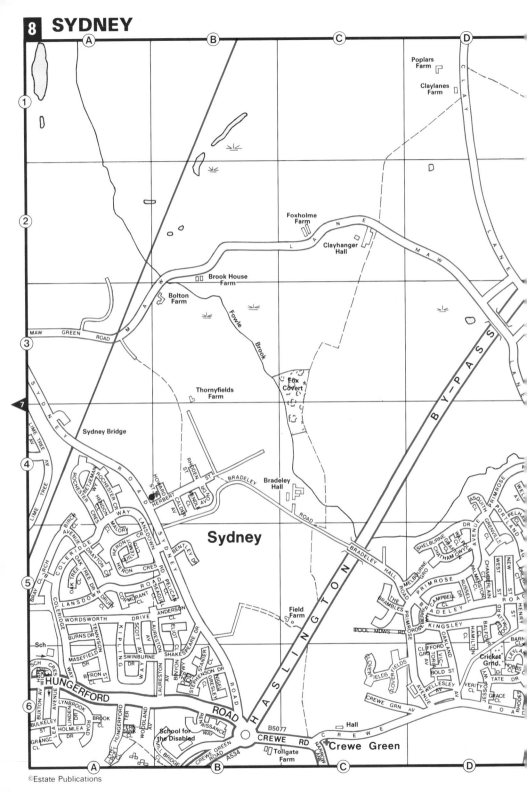

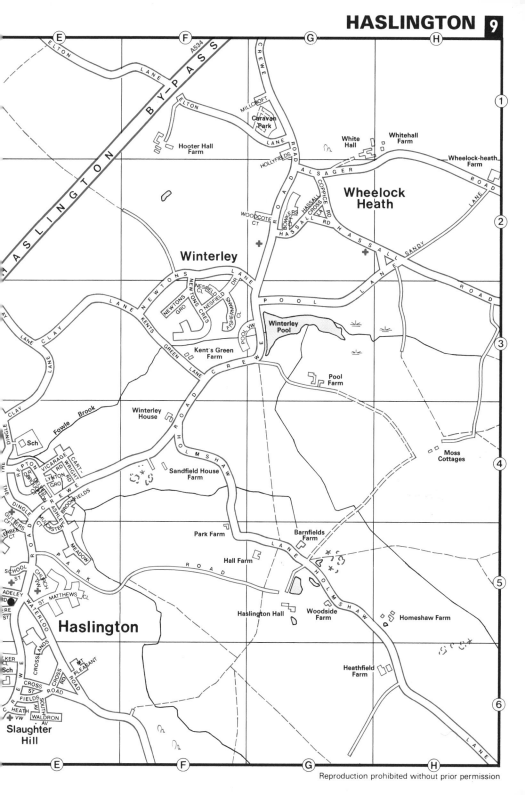

E F G H

1
2
3
4
5
6

A534

HASLINGTON BY-PASS

ELTON LANE

ELTON LANE

CREWE

MILLCROFT

Caravan Park

LANE

Hooter Hall Farm

HOLLYFIELDS

WOODCOTE CT

ROAD

ALSAGER

COPPICE RD

HASSALL CROSS

BOWKERS

HASSALL

ROAD

HASSALL RD

White Hall

Whitehall Farm

Whitehall

Wheelock-heath Farm

ROAD

Wheelock Heath

LANE

SANDY

ROAD

Winterley

NEWTONS LANE

NESFIELD CL

NESFIELD

NEWTONS GRO

FISHERMANS DR

NEWTONS CRES

CL

POOL VW

POOL

Winterley Pool

CREWE

Kent's Green Farm

KENTS GREEN LANE

Pool Farm

AV

LANE

CLAY

LANE

Fowle Brook

Winterley House

CLAY

DINGLE

Sch

HEPTON OLD

VICARAGE

CART-WRIGHT

LYNTON GRO

RD

BROOKFIELDS

ROAD

CREWE

ROAD

Sandfield House Farm

HOLMSHAW

Moss Cottages

THE DINGLE

GUTTER'S CL

FERBEE CT

ASHLEY

UPCASTER

MEADOW

PARK

Park Farm

Hall Farm

ROAD

Barnfields Farm

HOLMSHAW LANE

SCHOOL ST

ADELEY

ERE ST

CHURCH VW

ST. MATTHEWS CL

Haslington

WATERLOO

ST

CROSSLANDS

CROSS RD

MT PLEASANT

CROSS ST

FIELDS

ROAD

SOUTH

HEATH VW

WALDRON AV

Slaughter Hill

KER CL

Sch

Haslington Hall

Woodside Farm

Homeshaw Farm

Heathfield Farm

HOLMSHAW LANE

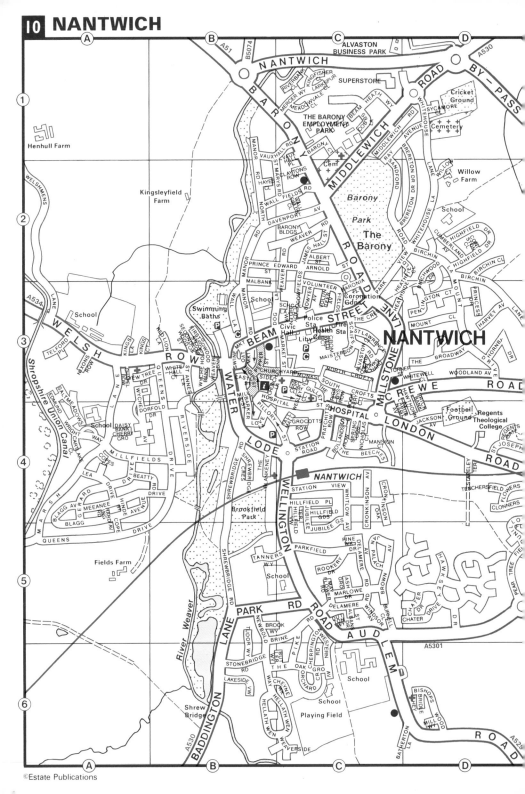

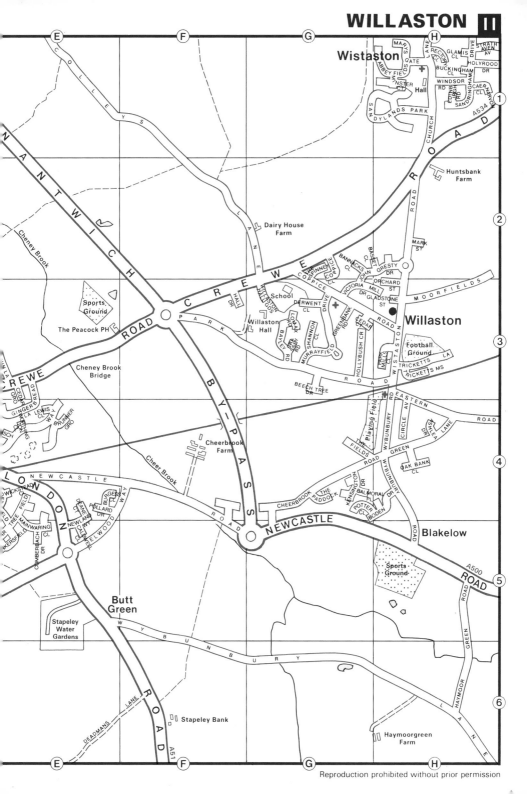

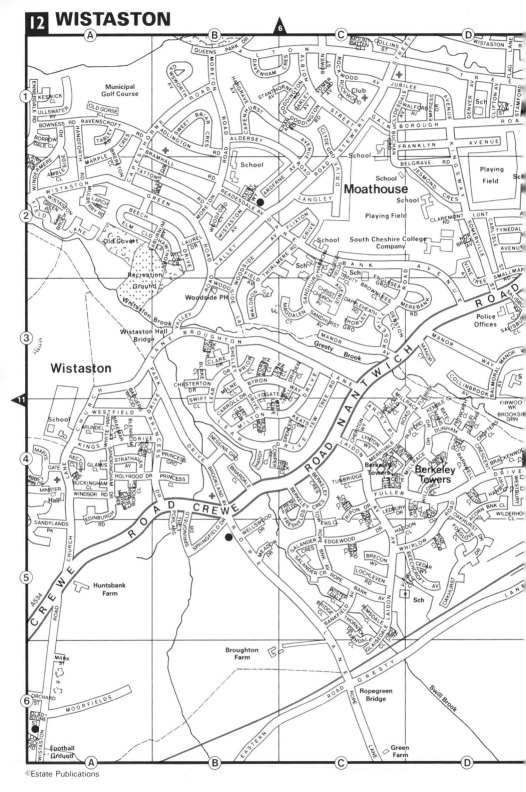

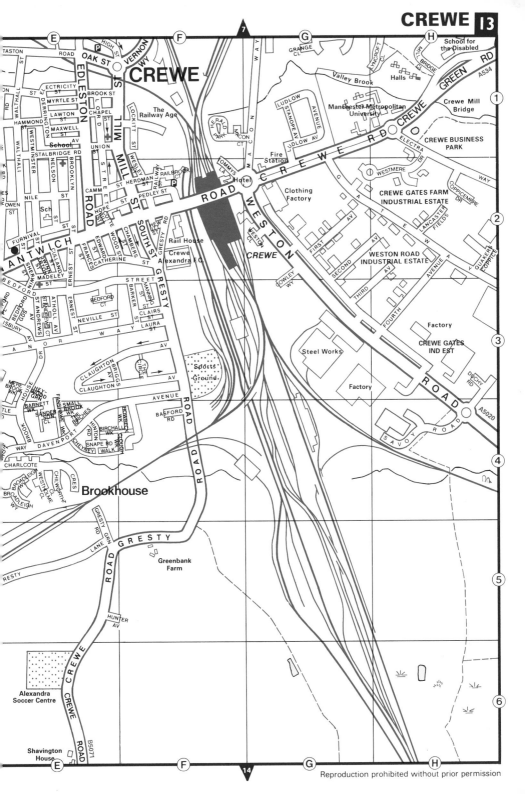

CREWE

7

E · F · G · H

School for the Disabled

Valley Brook

Halls

Crewe Mill Bridge

Manchester Metropolitan University

CREWE BUSINESS PARK

CREWE GATES FARM INDUSTRIAL ESTATE

WESTMERE

WESTON ROAD INDUSTRIAL ESTATE

Clothing Factory

Fire Station

Hotel

The Railway Age

School

Rail House

Crewe Alexandra F.C.

CREWE

Factory

CREWE GATES IND EST

Steel Works

Factory

A5020

Sports Ground

Brookhouse

Greenbank Farm

Alexandra Soccer Centre

Shavington House

14

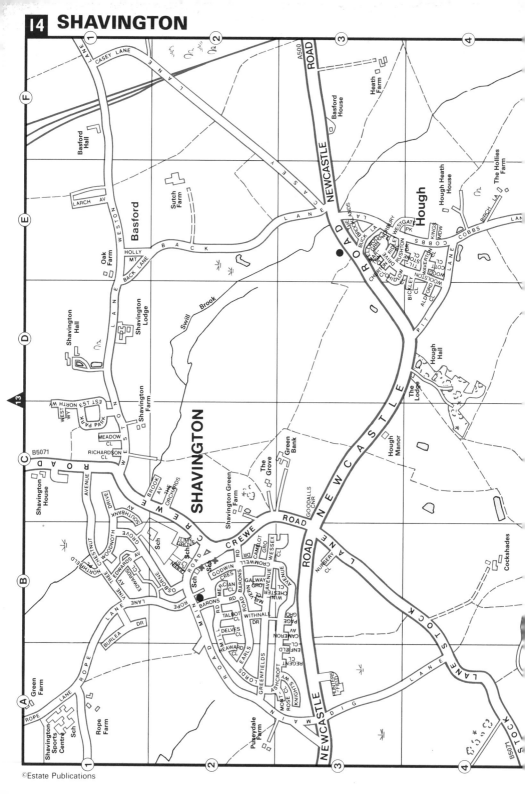

14 SHAVINGTON

©Estate Publications

A - Z INDEX TO STREETS
with Postcodes

The Index includes some names for which there is insufficient space on the maps. These names are preceded by an * and are followed by the nearest adjoining thoroughfare.

CREWE

Abbey Fields. CW2 — 12 A4
Abbey Pl. CW1 — 7 E5
Abbotsbury Clo. CW2 — 12 D4
Abingdon Clo. CW1 — 7 E3
Acacia Cres. CW1 — 7 H4
Acer Av. CW1 — 7 G3
Acorn Bank Clo. CW2 — 12 D4
Acton Rd. CW2 — 6 A5
Addison Clo. CW2 — 12 B4
Adelaide St. CW1 — 7 E5
Adlington Rd. CW2 — 12 B1
Alban St. CW1 — 7 E5
Albert St. CW1 — 7 F5
Albion St. CW2 — 12 C1
Aldersey Rd. CW2 — 12 B1
Aldford Clo. CW2 — 14 D4
Alexandra Pl. CW1 — 7 E4
Allen Pl. CW1 — 7 E5
Alma Av. CW1 — 7 F4
Almond Av. CW1 — 7 G3
Alsager Rd. CW11 — 9 G2
Alton St. CW2 — 12 B1
Alvaston Walk. CW2 — 12 B2
Ambleside Clo. CW2 — 12 A2
Ambuscade Clo. CW1 — 7 H5
Amy St. CW2 — 12 D1
Anderson Clo. CW1 — 8 B5
Arderne Av. CW2 — 12 B2
Ardleigh Clo. CW1 — 6 C2
Arley Pl. CW2 — 12 C4
*Arlington Clo,
Westbury Clo. CW2 — 12 D4
Arran Clo. CW2 — 6 A6
Artle Rd. CW2 — 13 E4
Arundel Clo. CW2 — 12 A4
Ash Rd. CW1 — 7 G3
Ashcroft Av. CW2 — 14 A3
Ashley Meadow. CW1 — 9 E4
Ashmuir Clo. CW1 — 7 E4
Ashville Ct. CW2 — 12 D5
Asquith Clo. CW1 — 8 D4
Astbury Clo. CW1 — 6 D2
Atholl Av. CW2 — 13 E3
Attwood Clo. CW1 — 8 D5
Audley St. CW1 — 7 G4
Audley St West. CW1 — 7 F4
Avon Dri. CW1 — 8 B4

Back La. CW2 — 14 E1
Badger Av. CW1 — 6 C4
Badgers Wood. CW2 — 12 A3
Bailey Clo. CW1 — 7 F3
Balfour Clo. CW1 — 8 D5
Balmoral Av. CW2 — 12 D3
Bankfield Av. CW2 — 12 C5
Barker St. CW2 — 13 F3
*Barleywood Clo,
Millrace Dri. CW2 — 12 D4
Barnabas Av. CW1 — 6 C4
Barnes Clo. CW1 — 8 D6
Barnett Walk. CW2 — 13 E4
Barnwell Clo. CW2 — 12 D4
Barons Rd. CW2 — 14 B2
Barrie Gro. CW1 — 7 H5
Barrows Clo. CW1 — 6 D2
Barthomley Cres. CW2 — 6 A5
Basford Rd. CW2 — 13 F4
Batemans Clo. CW2 — 12 D4
Batterbee Ct. CW1 — 9 E5
Beaumont Clo. CW2 — 12 B4

Becconsall Clo. CW1 — 6 D1
Becconsall Dri. CW1 — 6 D1
Beckford Clo. CW1 — 6 C2
Bedford Ct. CW2 — 13 E3
Bedford Gdns. CW2 — 13 E3
Bedford Pl. CW2 — 13 E3
Bedford St. CW2 — 13 E3
Beech Dri. CW2 — 12 A2
Beech Gro. CW1 — 7 H5
Beech St. CW1 — 7 F5
Beech St East. CW1 — 7 F5
*Beech St West,
Hightown. CW1 — 7 F5
Beechcroft Av. CW2 — 12 D5
Belgrave Rd. CW2 — 12 D2
Beltony Dri. CW1 — 6 D1
Bennett Clo. CW1 — 7 H5
Bentley Dri. CW1 — 8 B5
Berkeley Cres. CW2 — 12 C4
Betjeman Way. CW1 — 8 A4
Betley St. CW1 — 7 F6
Bexington Dri. CW1 — 7 E1
Bickley Clo. CW2 — 14 D4
Bidvale Way. CW1 — 7 F2
Bilton Way. CW2 — 6 B5
Binyon Way. CW1 — 8 B6
Birch Av. CW1 — 8 A5
Birch Clo. CW1 — 8 A4
Birch La. CW2 — 14 E4
Birchall Walk. CW2 — 13 E4
Birchmuir Clo. CW1 — 7 E3
Blackthorn Clo. CW2 — 12 C4
Blake Clo. CW2 — 12 B3
Bleasedale Rd. CW1 — 7 E1
Blenheim Clo. CW2 — 12 A4
Bodnant Clo. CW2 — 6 D2
Bold St. CW1 — 8 D6
Bolshaw Clo. CW1 — 6 D2
Borrowdale Clo. CW2 — 12 A1
Bowen Cooke Av. CW1 — 6 D4
Bowen St. CW2 — 12 C1
Bowkers Croft. CW11 — 9 G2
Bowland Croft. CW1 — 7 E1
Bowness Rd. CW2 — 12 A1
Brackenwood Clo. CW2 — 12 D4
Bradeley Hall Rd. CW1 — 8 C5
*Bradeley Rd,
Haslington. CW1 — 8 D5
Bradeley Rd, Sydney. CW1 — 8 B4
Bradfield Rd. CW1 — 6 C1
Braemar Clo. CW2 — 12 A4
Bramhall Rd. CW2 — 12 A1
Bray Clo. CW1 — 8 A5
Brecon Way. CW2 — 12 C5
Brereton Clo. CW2 — 12 A1
Briardale Clo. CW2 — 12 B4
Bridge Clo. CW2 — 12 C5
Bridle Rd. CW2 — 7 E6
Brierley St. CW1 — 7 G5
Briggs Av. CW2 — 13 E3
Bright St. CW1 — 7 E5
Broad St. CW1 — 7 F3
Broadleigh Way. CW2 — 13 E4
Bromley Clo. CW1 — 6 C2
Brook Av. CW2 — 14 C2
Brook Clo. CW1 — 8 A6
Brook St. CW2 — 13 E1
Brookdale Pk. CW2 — 6 D6
Brookfields. CW1 — 9 E4
Brookhouse Dri. CW2 — 13 E4
Brookland Av. CW2 — 12 B4
Brooklands Gro. CW1 — 6 D4
Brooklyn St. CW2 — 13 E2
Brookside Grn. CW2 — 12 D4
Broom St. CW2 — 6 D4
Broughton La. CW2 — 12 B3
Broughton Rd. CW1 — 7 F1
Brown Lees Clo. CW2 — 12 C3
Browning St. CW1 — 7 E5
Buchan Gro. CW2 — 12 C1
Buck La. CW2 — 14 E3

Buckingham Clo. CW2 — 12 A4
Bude Clo. CW1 — 7 E2
Bulkeley St. CW1 — 8 A6
Burjen Way. CW1 — 7 E4
Burlea Clo. CW2 — 6 B5
Burlea Dri. CW2 — 14 B1
Burns Dri. CW1 — 8 A5
Burton Gro. CW1 — 7 E1
Buttermere Dri. CW1 — 7 E1
Buxton Av. CW1 — 8 A6
Byron Clo. CW1 — 8 A6
Byron Way. CW2 — 12 B3

Caernarvon Rd. CW2 — 12 A4
Calder Av. CW1 — 8 B4
*Camden St,
Thomas St. CW1 — 7 G5
Camelot Gro. CW2 — 14 B2
Cameron Av. CW2 — 14 B3
Camm St. CW2 — 13 E2
Campbell Clo. CW1 — 8 D5
Canford Clo. CW1 — 7 E1
Capenhurst Av. CW2 — 12 B1
Capesthorne Rd. CW2 — 12 A2
Carisbrook Clo. CW2 — 12 A4
Carlisle St. CW2 — 12 D2
Carrington Way. CW1 — 7 E2
Carroll Dri. CW2 — 12 B4
Cartwright Rd. CW1 — 9 E4
Casey La. CW2 — 14 E3
Casson St. CW1 — 7 E5
Castle St. CW1 — 7 E6
Castlemere Dri. CW1 — 7 F3
Catherine St. CW2 — 13 E2
Cavendish Rd. CW2 — 6 B5
Cedar Way. CW2 — 12 D5
Chalfields Clo. CW2 — 12 D4
Chamberlain Ct. CW1 — 8 D5
Chambers St. CW2 — 13 F2
*Chantry Ct,
Prince Albert St. CW1 — 7 F6
Chapel St. CW2 — 13 E1
Chapelmere Ct. CW1 — 7 F3
*Charles St,
Victoria St. CW1 — 7 F5
Charlesworth St. CW1 — 7 G4
Charlcote Cres. CW2 — 13 E4
Chatham Way. CW1 — 8 D5
Chatsworth Clo. CW2 — 12 C4
Chell St. CW1 — 7 E4
Cheltenham Cres. CW1 — 7 E3
Cheriton Way. CW2 — 12 C4
Cherry Tree Rd. CW1 — 7 G3
Chester Sq. CW1 — 7 F6
Chester St. CW1 — 7 F6
Chesterton Dri. CW2 — 12 B3
Chestnut Av. CW2 — 14 B1
Chestnut Gro. CW1 — 7 H5
Chetwode St. CW1 — 7 F5
Cheyney Walk. CW2 — 13 E4
Chidlow Clo. CW2 — 14 E3
Chilworth Clo. CW2 — 13 E4
Christchurch Av. CW2 — 12 C3
Christleton Av. CW2 — 6 A5
Church La. CW2 — 12 A4
Church View. CW1 — 9 E5
*Church View Walk,
Church La. CW2 — 12 A4
Church Walk. CW2 — 12 A4
Churchmere Dri. CW1 — 7 F3
Churton Clo. CW2 — 14 E3
Clare Dri. CW2 — 12 B3
Claremont Rd. CW2 — 12 D2
Clarence Gro. CW1 — 7 E5
Claughton Av. CW2 — 13 E3
Clay La. CW1 — 8 D1
Clayton Clo. CW1 — 6 D2
Cliffe Rd. CW1 — 7 E2
Clifford Gro. CW1 — 8 D6
Clifton Av. CW2 — 12 D1
Clifton St. CW1 — 12 D1

Clough Walk. CW2 — 13 F4
Cloverfields. CW1 — 8 C6
Clyde Gro. CW2 — 12 C1
Clydesdale Av. CW2 — 12 C1
Cobbs La. CW2 — 14 E4
Coleridge Way. CW1 — 8 A5
College Fields. CW2 — 12 C2
Collinbrook Av. CW2 — 12 D3
Collins St. CW2 — 6 D6
Conrad Clo. CW1 — 7 H5
Conway Clo. CW1 — 7 E2
Coppenhall Gro. CW2 — 6 D6
Coppenhall Heyes. CW2 — 6 D6
Coppenhall La. CW2 — 6 A6
Coppice Rd. CW11 — 9 G2
Coppicemere Dri. CW1 — 13 H2
Cormorant Clo. CW1 — 8 A5
Cornwall Gro. CW1 — 7 E5
Coronation Cres. CW1 — 7 G4
Coronation St. CW1 — 7 G4
Cotterill St. CW2 — 13 E2
Cowley Way. CW1 — 13 G3
Cowper Clo. CW2 — 12 B4
Crab Tree Gro. CW1 — 7 H3
Cranage Rd. CW2 — 12 C1
Cranborne Rd. CW1 — 7 F4
Crane Brook Clo. CW1 — 6 D2
Crestwood Clo. CW2 — 12 D4
Crewe Grn Av. CW1 — 8 C6
Crewe Grn Rd. CW1 — 13 H1
Crewe Rd, Crewe. CW1 — 13 G2
Crewe Rd, Crewe Grn. CW1 — 8 B6
Crewe Rd, Haslington. CW1 — 9 E4
*Crewe Rd,
Shavington. CW2 — 14 B2
Crewe Rd, Wistaston. CW2 — 12 A5
Crewe St. CW1 — 7 G6
Crofters Clo. CW2 — 12 D4
Cromer Dri. CW1 — 7 E2
Cromwell Dri. CW2 — 14 B2
Cross Rd. CW1 — 9 E6
Cross St, Crewe. CW1 — 7 F6
Cross St, Haslington. CW1 — 9 E6
Crosslands. CW1 — 9 E6
Crossville St. CW1 — 7 G5
Crossway. CW1 — 7 F3
Culland St. CW2 — 13 E2
Cumberland Clo. CW1 — 7 G5

Dairyhouse Way. CW2 — 12 B2
Dale St. CW1 — 6 D4
Dane Bank Av. CW2 — 12 B2
Dapple Heath Rd. CW2 — 12 C3
Darley Av. CW2 — 12 C1
Darlington Av. CW1 — 6 C4
Davenham Cres. CW2 — 12 B1
Davenport Av. CW2 — 13 E4
Davenport St. CW1 — 7 F3
Delamere St. CW1 — 7 E6
Delves Broughton Ct. CW11 — 9 E4
Delves Clo. CW2 — 14 B2
Deneside Av. CW1 — 7 F3
Denston Clo. CW2 — 12 C3
Denver Av. CW2 — 12 D1
Derby St. CW1 — 7 E5
Derrington Av. CW1 — 13 E1
Deva Rd. CW2 — 6 B5
Dewes St. CW1 — 7 E5
Dig La. CW1 — 14 A3
Dillors Croft. CW1 — 6 D1
Doddington Rd. CW2 — 12 C1
Dorfold St. CW1 — 7 F6
Dorric Way. CW1 — 7 E3
Dovecote Clo. CW2 — 12 D4
Drayton Cres. CW1 — 8 A5
Drury Clo. CW1 — 8 A5
Dryden Clo. CW2 — 12 C3
Duchy Rd. CW1 — 13 H3
Duke St. CW2 — 13 E1
Dunham Cres. CW2 — 12 D4
Dunwoody Way. CW2 — 6 D5

Street	Ref	Street	Ref	Street	Ref	Street	Ref
Dutton Way. CW1	7 E4	Glamis Clo. CW2	12 A4	Hope St. CW2	13 E2	Lodgefields Dri. CW2	6 B6
		Glover St. CW1	6 D4	Hospital St. CW1	7 G4	*Longford St,	
Eadie Gro. CW1	6 D2	Goddard St. CW1	7 E5	Hothershall Clo. CW1	7 E1	Nantwich Clo. CW2	13 F2
Eardley Pl. CW1	7 E5	Godwin Cres. CW2	14 B2	Hove Clo. CW1	7 E2	Lord St. CW2	13 E1
Earle St. CW1	7 F6	Goldcrest Clo. CW1	6 C3	Howard St. CW1	8 B4	Lords Mill Rd. CW2	14 A2
Earls Rd. CW2	14 A2	Goodalls Cnr. CW2	14 C3	Howbeck Walk. CW2	13 F4	Ludford St. CW1	7 F5
Eastern Rd. CW2	12 B6	Goulden St. CW1	6 D4	Hughes Dri. CW2	6 C5	Ludlow Av. CW1	13 G1
Eaton St. CW2	7 F6	Grace Clo. CW1	8 D6	Hulme St. CW1	6 C5	Lunt Av. CW2	12 D2
Edgewood Dri. CW2	12 C5	Grafton Clo. CW	8 D5	Hungerford Av. CW1	7 H6	Lyceum Clo. CW1	6 D2
Edinburgh Rd. CW2	12 A5	Grand Junction Way. CW1	7 G6	Hungerford Rd. CW1	8 A6	Lyceum Way. CW1	7 E2
Edleston Dri. CW2	13 E1	Grange Clo. CW1	8 A6	Hungerford Ter. CW1	8 A6	Lydgate Clo. CW2	12 B3
Edward St. CW2	13 E2	Grasmere Av. CW2	6 C5	Hunter Av. CW2	13 E5	Lynbrook Rd. CW1	8 A6
Edwards Av. CW2	14 B1	Greenacres. CW1	7 F4	Huntersfield. CW2	14 A3	Lyncroft Clo. CW1	8 A6
Edwards Clo. CW2	14 B1	Greendale Gdns. CW1	7 H4	Hurn Clo. CW1	7 E1	Lynton Gro. CW1	9 E4
Eleanor Clo. CW1	6 C5	Greenfields Av. CW2	14 A2	Hythe Av. CW1	7 E1	Lynton Way. CW2	12 C4
Electra Way. CW1	13 H1	Greenway. CW1	7 F3			Lyon St. CW1	7 G6
Electricity St. CW2	13 E1	Grenville Clo. CW1	8 D5	**INDUSTRIAL ESTATES**			
Eliot Clo. CW1	8 B5	Gresty Grn Rd. CW2	13 E5	Crewe Business Pk. CW1	13 H1	Mablins La. CW1	7 E1
Elizabeth St. CW1	7 E5	Gresty La. CW2	12 C6	Crewe Gates Ind Est. CW1	13 H3	McLaren St. CW1	7 E3
*Ellesmere Pl,		Gresty Rd. CW2	13 F2	Crewe Gates		McNeill Av. CW1	6 C5
St Judes Clo. CW1	7 E4	Gresty Ter. CW1	7 H6	Farm Ind Est. CW1	13 H2	Macon Clo. CW1	13 F1
Ellis St. CW1	7 E3	Greystone Park. CW1	7 G5	Grand Junction Retail		Macon Way. CW1	7 H6
Ellwood Grn. CW2	14 E3	Groby Rd. CW1	7 G1	Park. CW1	7 G6	Madeley St. CW2	13 E2
Elm Clo. CW2	12 A2	Grosvenor St. CW1	7 E5	Weston Rd Ind Est. CW1	13 H2	Magdalan Ct. CW2	12 C3
Elm Dri. CW1	7 G4	Guillemot Clo. CW1	8 A5			Main Rd. CW2	14 A3
Elmstead Cres. CW1	6 C2	Gutterscroft. CW1	9 E4	Jackson St. CW1	6 D4	Malbank Rd. CW2	6 B5
Elton La. CW11	9 E1			James Atkinson Clo. CW1	6 C2	Malory Clo. CW2	8 A5
Empress Dri. CW2	12 D1	Haddon Clo. CW2	12 C5	Jesmond Cres. CW2	12 D2	Malvern Clo. CW2	14 B2
Enfield Clo. CW2	14 A3	Hall O Shaw St. CW1	7 G5	Jessop Way. CW2	8 D6	Manning St. CW2	13 F3
Englefield Clo. CW1	6 D2	Hallshaw Av. CW1	7 H5	John St. CW1	7 F5	Manor Av. CW2	12 C3
Englesea Gro. CW2	12 C3	Halton Dri. CW2	6 A5	Jubilee Av. CW2	12 C1	Manor Ct. CW2	12 C3
Ennerdale Rd. CW2	12 A1	Hamilton Clo. CW1	8 D5			Manor Way. CW2	12 D3
Ernest St. CW2	13 E3	Hammond St. CW2	13 E1	Keats Dri. CW2	12 C4	Maple Gro. CW1	7 G3
Evans St. CW1	7 E3	Hanbury Clo. CW2	12 D4	Kemble Clo. CW2	12 D4	March St. CW1	7 G5
		Handforth Rd. CW2	12 A1	Kempton Av. CW1	7 F3	Market Sq. CW1	7 F6
Fairbrook. CW2	12 A2	Harding St. CW1	7 G5	Kenilworth Clo. CW2	12 C4	Market St. CW1	7 F5
Fairburn Av. CW2	6 C5	Hardwicke Ct. CW1	8 A6	Kents Green La. CW1	9 F3	Market St. CW1	7 F6
Falcon Dri. CW1	7 E2	Hardy Clo. CW2	12 B4	Kents La. CW1	7 F1	Marlborough Clo. CW2	12 A4
Fallowfield Ct. CW1	6 D4	Hargrave Av. CW2	12 B1	Kestrel Dri. CW1	7 E2	Marley Av. CW1	7 E3
Falmouth Rd. CW1	6 D3	*Harrier Clo,		Keswick Clo. CW2	12 A1	Marlowe Clo. CW2	12 B4
Fanshawe Walk. CW2	13 E4	Rolls Av. CW2	6 C3	Kettell Av. CW1	6 C4	Marple Cres. CW2	12 A1
Farmer Clo. CW2	6 D5	Harris Clo. CW1	7 E1	Kinder Dri. CW2	6 A6	Marshfield Av. CW2	6 A5
Farmleigh Clo. CW1	6 C2	Harrow Clo. CW2	12 C2	King St. CW1	7 G6	Marshfield Bank. CW2	6 A6
Farmleigh Dri. CW1	6 C2	Haslemere Way. CW1	7 F4	Kings Dri. CW2	12 A4	Marton Clo. CW2	14 E3
Farndale Clo. CW2	12 C5	Haslington By-Pass. CW1	8 B6	Kings Meadow. CW2	14 E4	Mary St. CW1	7 G5
Fern Ct. CW1	7 H6	Hassall Cross La. CW11	9 G2	*Kingfisher Clo,		Marys Gate. CW2	12 A4
Fernbank Clo. CW1	8 A6	Hassall Rd. CW11	9 G2	Leighton Park. CW1	6 C3	Masefield Dri. CW1	8 A6
Field Av. CW2	12 B2	Haweswater Av. CW1	7 E1	Kingsley Rd. CW1	8 D5	Mavor Ct. CW1	7 E6
Field La. CW2	12 A2	Hawthorn Av. CW1	7 G3	Kingsway. CW2	12 D2	Maw Grn. CW1	7 H3
Fields Rd. CW1	9 E6	Hawthorn La. CW2	12 B2	Kinloch Clo. CW1	7 E4	Maw Green Rd. CW1	7 H3
Firbeck Gdns. CW2	6 A6	Hayling Clo. CW1	7 E1	Kipling Way. CW1	8 A5	Maw La. CW1	8 A3
First Av. CW1	13 G2	Hazel Gro. CW1	7 F3	Knights Way. CW2	14 A3	Maxwell St. CW2	13 E1
Firwood Walk. CW2	12 D4	Healey Clo. CW1	6 D2			Mayfield Mews. CW1	6 C3
Fishermans Clo. CW11	9 F3	Heath St. CW1	7 F5	Laburnum Av. CW2	12 B2	Meadow Clo. CW2	14 C1
Flag La. CW1	7 E6	Heath View. CW1	9 E6	Laburnum Gro. CW1	7 G4	Meadow Dri. CW2	12 B5
Flamingo Clo. CW2	6 C3	Heathergate Pl. CW2	12 C4	Laidon Av. CW2	12 C4	Melbourne Gro. CW1	8 D5
Fletcher St. CW1	7 E5	Heathfield Av. CW1	7 E5	Lambourne Dri. CW1	6 D1	Mellor St. CW1	7 G4
Flixton Dri. CW2	12 C2	Heaward Clo. CW2	14 A2	Lancaster Fields. CW1	13 H2	Melrose Dri. CW1	7 E1
Flowers La. CW1	6 C1	Helford Clo. CW2	13 E4	Langdale Rd. CW2	12 A1	Melrose Way. CW1	7 E2
Ford Clo. CW1	7 E4	Helmsdale Clo. CW1	7 E3	Langley Dri. CW2	13 C2	Mercian Clo. CW2	14 B2
Ford La. CW1	7 E4	Hendon Clo. CW1	8 A4	Lansdown Rd. CW1	8 A5	Mere Clo. CW1	9 E5
Forge St. CW1	7 G6	Henry St, Crewe. CW1	7 G5	Larch Av. CW2	14 E1	Mere St. CW1	9 E5
Foulkes Av. CW1	6 C4	Henry St, Haslington. CW1	8 D5	Larch Rd. CW2	12 A2	Merebank Rd. CW2	12 C3
Four Seasons Clo. CW2	12 D4	Herald Park, CW1	13 F1	Latimer Dri. CW1	6 D5	Merebrook Walk. CW2	13 E3
Fourth Av. CW1	13 H3	Herbert St. CW1	8 B4	Laura St. CW2	13 F3	Meredith St. CW1	7 F5
Foxes Hollow. CW1	7 H3	Herdman St. CW2	13 F2	Laurel Dri. CW2	12 B2	Merganser Clo. CW1	6 C3
Foxglove Clo. CW2	12 D5	Heron Cres. CW1	8 A5	Laureston Av. CW1	8 B6	Merlin Way. CW1	6 D2
Frances St. CW2	13 E2	Herrick Clo. CW2	12 C4	Lawford Clo. CW1	6 C2	Merrills Av. CW2	6 B5
Frank Bott Av. CW1	6 D2	Hesketh Croft. CW1	6 D1	Lawrence St. CW1	7 F6	Merrivale Rd. CW2	12 C4
Frank Webb Av. CW1	6 D3	Hewitt St. CW2	13 F2	Lawton St. CW2	13 E1	Meynell Clo. CW2	12 C4
Franklyn Av. CW2	12 C1	Heywood Grn. CW2	13 E3	Lea Av. CW1	8 A6	Micklewright Av. CW1	7 G4
Freshfields. CW2	12 C4	Hidcote Clo. CW2	12 C4	Lear Dri. CW2	12 B3	Middlewich Rd. CW1	6 B1
Fulbeck Clo. CW2	12 D4	High St. CW2	7 F6	Ledbury Dri. CW2	12 C4	Middlewich St. CW1	7 G3
Fuller Dri. CW2	12 C4	Highgate Clo. CW1	6 D2	Leighton Park. CW1	6 C3	Mill Bridge Clo. CW	8 B6
Fulmar Ct. CW1	6 C3	Hightown. CW1	7 F5	*Leighton St,		Mill St. CW2	13 F1
Furber St. CW1	7 F5	Hill St. CW1	7 G5	Underwood La. CW1	6 D4	Millcroft. CW11	9 F1
Furnival St. CW2	13 E2	Hillside Dri. CW1	7 H5	Leighton View. CW1	6 D2	Millrace Dri. CW2	12 D4
		Hinton Rd. CW2	13 E4	Lewis St. CW2	7 E6	Mills Way. CW1	7 E1
Gainsborough Rd. CW2	12 C1	Hobbs Clo. CW1	8 D6	Leyland Gro. CW1	8 D6	Milne Clo. CW2	12 B3
Galway Gro. CW2	14 B2	Holbury Clo. CW1	7 E1	Lime Gro. CW2	14 B2	Milton Dri. CW2	12 B4
Gatefield St. CW1	7 F5	Holland St. CW1	7 E3	Lime St. CW2	7 F3	Minshull New Rd. CW1	6 C1
Gateway. CW1	13 G2	Holly Mount. CW2	14 E1	Lime Tree Av. CW1	7 G3	Minster Ct. CW2	12 A4
Gawsworth Av. CW2	12 B1	Hollyfields. CW11	9 G2	Lincoln St. CW1	7 E5	Mirion St. CW1	7 G5
Gillow Clo. CW1	6 D2	Holmlea Dri. CW1	8 A6	Linden Dri. CW1	8 A6	Moathouse Dri. CW2	12 C2
*Gladstone St,		Holmshaw La. CW1	9 F4	Lingfield Dri. CW1	7 E3	Monk St. CW1	6 D5
Beech Clo. CW1	7 E2	Holt St. CW1	7 E5	Linnet Clo. CW1	8 A6	Monks La. CW1	6 C4
Glaisedale Clo. CW2	12 C5	Holyrood Dri. CW2	12 A4	Lockitt St. CW2	13 F1	Montrose Clo. CW2	14 A3

16

Moreton Rd. CW2	12 B1	Pool Meadows Rd. CW1	8 C5	St Matthews Clo. CW1	9 E5	Tabley Rd. CW2	12 A1

Moreton Rd. CW2 12 B1
Morgan Clo. CW2 6 D6
Moss Croft. CW1 6 D2
Moss Dale Clo. CW2 6 B6
Moss La. CW1 6 D1
*Moss Sq,
   Prince Albert St. CW1 7 F6
Mossford Av. CW1 7 E2
Mount Pleasant,
   Crewe. CW1 7 E4
Mount Pleasant,
   Haslington. CW1 9 E6
Mountbatten Ct. CW2 6 D6
Mulberry Rd. CW2 12 A2
Mulcaster Ct. CW1 9 E5
Myrtle St. CW2 13 E1

Nantwich Rd. CW2 12 C4
Narrow La. CW1 8 C6
Nelson St. CW2 13 E2
Nesfield Clo. CW11 9 F3
Nesfield Dri. CW11 9 F3
Nessina Gro. CW2 12 B4
Neville St. CW2 13 E3
Nevis Dri. CW2 6 A6
New St. CW1 8 D5
Newcastle Rd. CW2 14 A3
Newcastle St. CW1 6 D4
Newdigate St. CW1 7 F5
Newfield Dri. CW1 7 G5
Newton St. CW1 7 F5
Newtons Cres. CW11 9 F3
Newtons Gro. CW11 9 F3
Newtons La. CW11 9 F3
Nigel Gresley Clo. CW1 8 B6
Nghtingale Clo. CW1 6 C3
Nile St. CW2 13 E2
Nixon St. CW1 6 C5
Norbreck Av. CW2 12 D2
Norbury Clo. CW2 14 E3
*North Stafford St,
   Thomas St. CW1 7 G5
North St. CW1 7 F2
North Way. CW2 14 C1
Northfield Pl. CW2 14 B1
Nursery Clo. CW2 14 B3
Nutfield Av. CW1 7 E2

Oak St. CW2 7 F6
Oak Tree Clo. CW1 8 A5
Oak Tree Dri. CW1 8 A5
Oakhurst Dri. CW2 12 D5
Oakland Av. CW1 8 D6
Oakley St. CW1 7 F5
Oakwood Cres. CW2 6 B6
Old Gorse Clo. CW2 12 A1
Orchard Ct. CW1 8 D5
Orchard St. CW1 7 E5
Osborne Gro. CW2 14 B2
Owen St. CW2 13 E2
Oxford St. CW1 7 E5

Padmore Clo. CW1 6 C3
Padstow Clo. CW1 7 E2
Page Gro. CW2 14 B3
Palmerston Clo. CW1 8 D5
Park Dri. CW2 12 B3
Park Est. CW2 14 C1
Park Rd. CW1 9 E5
Parkers Rd. CW1 6 D1
Parkfield. CW1 6 D1
Parkstone Dri. CW1 7 E1
Pear Tree Av. CW1 7 E2
Pedley St. CW2 13 F2
Peel Sq. CW1 7 E5
Peel St. CW1 7 E5
Pelham Clo. CW1 8 D4
Pelican Clo. CW1 8 B5
Penbrook Clo. CW1 6 A6
Pendle Clo. CW1 8 B4
Peter Pl. CW1 7 E5
Petworth Clo. CW2 12 D5
Pinewood Ct. CW2 12 D5
Pit La. CW2 14 D4
Plane Tree Dri. CW1 7 G4
Pool La. CW11 9 G3

Pool Meadows Rd. CW1 8 C5
Pool View. CW11 9 F3
Poplar Gro. CW1 7 H5
Portland Gro. CW1 8 D4
Preece Ct. CW1 7 E5
Primrose Av. CW1 8 D4
Primrose Hill. CW2 6 B5
Prince Albert St. CW1 7 F6
Princess Clo. CW2 12 B4
Princess Dri. CW2 12 B4
Princess Gro. CW2 12 B4
Princess St. CW1 7 E4
Prior Clo. CW2 12 B3
Priory Clo. CW1 6 D2
Priscilla St. CW1 7 G6
Probert Clo. CW2 6 D5
Prunus Rd. CW1 7 G4
Pyms La. CW1 6 A4
Pyrus Av. CW1 7 H4

Quakers Coppice. CW1 13 H2
Queen St, Crewe. CW1 7 G5
Queen St,
   Shavington. CW2 14 B2
Queens Park Dri. CW2 6 C6
Queens Park Gdns. CW2 6 C5
Queensway. CW1 7 F6

Railbrook Ct. CW2 13 F2
Railton Av. CW1 6 D3
Railway St. CW2 13 F2
Rainbow St. CW1 7 G6
*Ramsbottom St,
   Clarence Gro. CW1 7 E5
Ravenscroft Rd. CW2 12 A1
Readesdale Av. CW2 12 B2
Rectory Clo. CW2 12 A4
Regent Clo. CW2 14 A3
Reid St. CW1 7 F4
Remer St. CW1 7 G3
*Renaissance Ct,
   Renaissance Way. CW1 8 B6
Renaissance Way. CW1 8 B6
Repton Dri. CW1 9 E4
Rhoden St. CW1 8 B4
Rhodes Clo. CW1 8 D6
Richard Moon St. CW1 7 E5
Richard St. CW1 7 E5
Richardson Clo. CW2 14 C1
Richmond Rd. CW1 7 H5
Ridgway St. CW1 7 G4
Ridley Clo. CW2 14 E3
Rigby Av. CW1 6 D2
Rigg St. CW1 7 E5
Rimsdale Clo. CW2 12 C5
Ripon Dri. CW2 12 C4
Rochester Cres. CW1 8 A4
Rockwood Av. CW2 12 C1
Rockwood Clo. CW2 12 C1
*Roebuck St,
   Broad St. CW1 7 F5
Roedean Walk. CW1 7 F4
Rolls Av. CW1 6 D3
Rook St. CW2 13 E2
Rope Bank Av. CW2 12 C5
Rope La. CW2 12 B5
Rose Ter. CW1 7 F5
Roseberry Way. CW1 8 D5
Rosehill Rd. CW2 12 C3
Rosewood Clo. CW1 7 H4
Rowton Rd. CW2 6 A5
Royce Clo. CW1 6 D3
Rudheath Clo. CW2 6 B5
Rufford Clo. CW2 12 D4
Ruskin Rd. CW2 13 E1
Russell Dri. CW1 8 D5
Rydal Mt. CW1 7 E1
Ryde Clo. CW1 7 E2
Ryebank Av. CW1 7 E3

St Andrews Av. CW2 13 E3
St Andrews Ct. CW2 13 E3
St Clairs St. CW2 13 F3
*St John St,
   Victoria St. CW1 7 F5
St Judes Clo. CW1 7 E4
St Marys St. CW1 7 F6

St Matthews Clo. CW1 9 E5
St Michaels View. CW1 7 E4
St Pauls Clo. CW1 7 F5
*St Pauls St,
   Victoria St. CW1 7 F5
Salander Cres. CW2 12 C4
Salisbury Av. CW2 12 D3
Salisbury Clo. CW2 12 D3
Samuel St. CW1 7 E5
Sanderson Clo. CW2 13 E4
Sandhurst Av. CW2 12 C3
Sandiway Rd. CW1 6 D3
Sandon Park Gdns. CW2 6 B6
Sandon St. CW1 7 F6
Sandown Rd. CW1 7 F2
Sandpiper Clo. CW1 6 C3
Sandringham Dri. CW2 12 A4
Sandy La. CW11 9 H2
Sandylands Pk. CW2 12 A5
*Saunders St,
   Browning St. CW1 7 E5
Savoy Rd. CW1 13 H4
School Cres. CW1 8 A6
School St. CW1 9 E5
Scott Av. CW1 8 A5
Seagull Clo. CW1 8 B5
Seaton Clo. CW1 7 E2
Second Av. CW1 13 G2
Sedgemere Av. CW1 6 D2
Selsey Clo. CW1 7 E2
Selworthy Dri. CW1 7 E2
Shakespeare Dri. CW1 8 B6
Sharnbrook Dri. CW2 6 B6
Shelburne Dri. CW1 8 D5
Shelley Dri. CW2 12 B3
Sheppard St. CW1 7 G5
Sherborne Rd. CW1 7 F4
Sheridan Clo. CW1 7 E1
Sheringham Dri. CW1 7 E2
Sherwin St. CW2 13 E2
Simpson Clo. CW1 7 E1
Singleton Av. CW1 7 F4
Skylark Clo. CW1 6 C3
Smallbrook Walk. CW2 13 E4
Smallman Rd. CW2 12 D2
Smith Gro. CW1 6 C4
Smithy La. CW2 6 B2
Snape Rd. CW2 13 E4
Snowdon Dri. CW2 6 A6
Somerford Av. CW2 12 C1
Somerley Clo. CW1 7 E1
Somerville St. CW2 12 D2
Sorbus Dri. CW1 7 G4
South Av. CW1 9 E6
South St. CW2 13 F2
Southbank Av. CW1 14 C1
Spencer Clo. CW2 12 C4
Spring Gdns. CW1 7 G5
Springfield Dri. CW2 12 B5
Springwell Dri. CW2 12 D4
Stafford St. CW1 7 E5
Stalbridge Rd. CW2 13 E1
Stamford Av. CW2 12 D1
Stamp Av. CW1 7 G3
Stanhope Av. CW1 13 G1
Stanier Clo. CW1 8 B6
Stanley St. CW1 7 F6
Stanthorne Av. CW2 12 C1
Stephenson Dri. CW1 8 B6
Stewart St. CW2 12 C1
Stock La. CW2 14 A4
Stonechat Clo. CW1 6 C3
Stoneley Av. CW1 7 F2
Stoneley Rd. CW1 7 F2
Strathaven Av. CW2 12 A4
Sunart Clo. CW2 12 C5
Sundale Dri. CW2 6 A6
Sunnybank Rd. CW2 6 B5
Surrey St. CW1 7 H5
Swallowfield Clo. CW2 12 C4
Sweet Briar Cres. CW2 12 B1
Swift Clo. CW2 12 B4
Swinburne Dri. CW1 8 A6
Swinnerton St. CW2 13 E2
Sycamore Av. CW1 7 G3
Sydney Rd. CW1 8 A3

Tabley Rd. CW2 12 A1
Talbot Clo. CW2 14 B2
Tarvin Av. CW2 6 A5
Tate Dri. CW1 8 D6
Tatton Rd. CW2 12 A2
Tennyson Clo. CW2 12 B3
Tennyson St. CW1 8 A5
The Birches. CW2 13 E4
The Brambles. CW1 8 C5
The Brooklands. CW2 14 E3
The Circle. CW2 13 F3
The Dingle. CW1 9 E4
The Haven. CW1 7 G3
The Orchards. CW2 14 C2
The Poplars. CW2 12 b4
The Retreat. CW1 7 F3
Third Av. CW1 13 G3
Thirlmere Rd. CW2 12 B2
Thomas St. CW1 7 G5
Thorley Gro. CW2 12 C3
Thorn Tree Dri. CW1 6 D1
Thornton Dri. CW2 12 C5
Thorpe Clo. CW1 6 C2
Tilstone Clo. CW2 14 E4
Timbrell Av. CW1 6 C4
Tollemache Dri. CW1 6 D2
Tollitt St. CW1 7 F6
Tomkinson Clo. CW1 6 C3
Tommys La. CW1 13 F2
Tower Way. CW1 7 F7
Towers Clo. CW2 12 C4
Trevithick Clo. CW1 8 B6
Trinity Clo. CW2 12 C2
Tunbridge Clo. CW1 12 C4
Turner Clo. CW2 6 C2
Tynedale Av. CW2 12 D2

Ullswater Av. CW2 12 A1
Underwood La. CW1 6 D4
Union St. CW2 13 E1
Unnet Clo. CW1 6 D3

Valley Rd. CW2 12 B2
Verdin Ct. CW1 6 D1
Verity Clo. CW1 8 D6
*Vernon St,
   Underwood La. CW1 6 D4
Vernon Way. CW1 7 F5
Vicarage Rd. CW1 9 E4
Victoria Av,
   Haslington. CW1 8 D6
Victoria Av,
   Lodgefields. CW2 6 B5
Victoria St. CW1 7 F5
Villiers Russell Clo. CW1 7 G5
Vincent St. CW1 7 H5
Vine Tree Av, Crewe. CW2 12 D2
Vine Tree Av,
   Shavington. CW2 14 B1

Waine St. CW1 7 G4
Wakefield Clo. CW1 6 C3
Waldron Av. CW1 9 E6
Waldron Gdns. CW2 12 B3
Waldrons La. CW1 7 F1
Walford Av. CW2 12 D1
Walker Clo. CW1 9 E6
Walker St. CW1 7 E4
Wallis St. CW1 7 G5
Walpole Clo. CW1 8 D5
Walthall St. CW2 13 E1
Wareham Dri. CW1 7 E2
Warrington Av. CW1 7 F3
Wasdale Gro. CW1 7 E1
Waterloo Rd. CW1 9 E5
Waverton Clo. CW2 14 E4
Wellcroft Clo. CW2 12 D4
Wellesley Av. CW1 8 D6
Wells Av. CW1 8 D4
Wellswood Dri. CW2 12 B5
Wesley Clo. CW2 13 F2
Wessex Clo. CW2 14 B2
West Av. CW1 7 E5
West St, Crewe. CW1 6 B5
West St, Haslington. CW1 8 D5
West Way. CW2 14 C1
Westbourne Av. CW1 6 D3

Westbury Clo. CW2 12 D4
Westfield Dri. CW2 12 A4
Westgate Pk. CW2 14 E3
Westholme Clo. CW2 13 E4
Westmere Dri. CW1 13 H2
Westminster St. CW2 13 E1
Weston Clo. CW1 13 G2
Weston La. CW2 14 C1
Weston Rd. CW1 13 G2
Wharfdale Av. CW1 7 E1
Wheatley Rd. CW1 7 H3
Wheelman Rd. CW1 6 D3
Whirlow Rd. CW2 12 D5
Whitby Clo. CW1 7 E2
White Av. CW2 6 C5
White Hart La. CW2 12 A4
Whittaker Clo. CW1 6 D3
Wilderhope Clo. CW2 12 D4
Wilding St. CW1 7 H6
Willow Cres. CW2 12 B2
Willows Clo. CW2 12 D4
Winchester Clo. CW2 14 B3
Windermere Rd. CW2 12 A2
Windsor Av. CW1 6 D3
Windsor Rd. CW2 12 A4
Wistaston Av. CW2 12 B2
Wistaston Green Rd. CW2 12 A2
Wistaston Park. CW2 12 B3
Wistaston Rd. CW2 7 E6
Wisterdale Clo. CW2 12 C5
Witham Clo. CW2 12 C4
Withnall Dri. CW2 14 B2
Wood St. CW2 13 E2
Woodbank Clo. CW2 12 C5
Woodcote Ct. CW11 9 G2
Woodcott Clo. CW2 14 E4
Woodford Clo. CW2 12 B2
Woodland Av. CW1 8 A6
Woodland Gdns. CW1 7 G4
Woodnoth Dri. CW2 14 B1
Woodside Av. CW2 12 B3
Woodside La. CW2 12 B3
Woolston Dri. CW2 14 D4
Wordsworth Clo. CW2 12 B3
Wordsworth Dri. CW1 8 A5
Wren Clo. CW1 6 C3

Yates St. CW2 12 D2
Yew Tree Rd. CW2 12 C4

NANTWICH

Albert St. CW5 10 C2
Alvaston Rd. CW5 10 C3
Arnold St. CW5 10 C2
Ash Gro. CW5 10 C5
Ashlea Dri. CW5 11 H4
Audlem Rd. CW5 10 C5
Baddington La. CW5 10 B6
Balmoral Pl. CW5 11 G4
Bannacks Clo. CW5 11 G2
Barker St. CW5 10 B4
Baronia Pl. CW5 10 C3
Barony Bldgs. CW5 10 C2
Barony Ct. CW5 10 C1
Barony Rd. CW5 10 B1
*Barony Ter,
  James Hall St. CW5 10 C2
Basset Clo. CW5 11 G2
Batherton La. CW5 10 D6
Bayley Rd. CW5 11 G3
Beam Heath Way. CW5 10 C1
Beam St. CW5 10 B3
Beatty Rd. CW5 10 A4
Beech Tree Dri. CW5 11 G3
Birchin Clo. CW5 10 D2
Birchin La. CW5 10 D2
Birchwood Dri. CW5 10 D2
Bishops Wood. CW5 10 D6
Blagg Av. CW5 10 A4
Boden Dri. CW5 11 G4
Bollands Row. CW5 10 C4
*Bowling Green Ct,
  Wesley Clo. CW5 10 C3

*Bowling Green Mews,
  Rectory Clo. CW5 10 C3
Bowyer Av. CW5 10 C3
Brassey Rd. CW5 11 G3
Brereton Dri. CW5 10 D2
Brick Bank. CW5 10 D3
Bridle Hey. CW5 10 D6
Brine Rd. CW5 10 C5
Brook Way. CW5 10 B5
Brown Av. CW5 10 C5
Brunner Gro. CW5 11 E4
Burgess Clo. CW5 11 E4
Burnell Clo. CW5 10 C5
Butler Clo. CW5 10 C6
Caldwell Clo. CW5 11 E5
Cartlake Clo. CW5 10 A4
Castle St. CW5 10 B3
Cedar Ct. CW5 11 G3
Cedar Gro. CW5 11 E3
*Chapel Mews,
  Market St. CW5 10 C3
Chapel Row. CW5 10 A3
Chater Dri. CW5 10 D5
Cheerbrook Rd. CW5 11 G4
Cherrington Rd. CW5 10 C6
Cherry Gro. CW5 10 A4
Cheyne Walk. CW5 10 C6
Church La. CW5 10 B3
Churchyardside. CW5 10 B3
Circle Av. CW5 11 H4
Claytons Row. CW5 10 C2
Cobbs La. CW5 10 C1
Colleys La. CW5 11 E1
Comberbach Dri. CW5 11 E5
Coniston Clo. CW5 10 D2
Cope St. CW5 10 A5
Copes La. CW5 10 A4
Coppice Clo. CW5 11 G2
Coppice Rd. CW5 11 G2
Cowfields. CW5 10 C3
Crewe Rd. CW5 10 C3
Cromwell Ct. CW5 10 C3
Cronkinson Av. CW5 10 C4
Cronkinson Oak. CW5 10 C4
Cross Wood St. CW5 10 B3
Cumberland Av. CW5 10 D2
Daisy Bank. CW5 10 A4
Davenport Av. CW5 10 B2
Deadmans La. CW5 11 E6
Deane Ct. CW5 11 E4
Delamere Rd. CW5 10 C5
Derwent Clo. CW5 11 G3
Dog La. CW5 10 B3
Dorfold Dri. CW5 10 A4
Dunillow Field. CW5 10 D5
Dutton Way. CW5 10 C5
Eastern Rd. CW5 11 H3
Edmund Wright Way. CW5 10 A3
Elwood Way. CW5 11 E5
First Wood St. CW5 10 B3
Flowers Croft. CW5 10 D4
Gerard Dri. CW5 10 A4
Gingerbread La. CW5 11 E3
Gladstone St. CW5 11 H3
Green La. CW5 11 H4
Greenbank Rd. CW5 11 G3
Grocotts Row. CW5 10 C4
Hall Dri. CW5 11 F3
Harding Rd. CW5 10 A4
Harvey Av. CW5 10 B2
Hawksey Dri. CW5 10 D5
Hawthorn Av. CW5 10 D3
Hayes Clo. CW5 10 B2
Haymoor Green Rd. CW5 11 H6
Heathfield Clo. CW5 10 D2
Heathside. CW5 10 C3
Hellath Wen. CW5 10 B6
High St. CW5 10 B3
Highfield Dri. CW5 10 D2
Hillfield Gdns. CW5 10 C4
Hillfield Pl. CW5 10 C4
Hillfield View. CW5 10 C4
Hinde St. CW5 10 A4
Hirsch Clo. CW5 11 E4
Hollybush Cres. CW5 11 G3
Hornby Dri. CW5 10 D3
Hospital St. CW5 10 C4

INDUSTRIAL & RETAIL:
Alvaston
  Business Pk. CW5 10 C1
The Barony
  Employment Pk. CW5 10 C1
Jackson Av. CW5 10 D4
James Hall St. CW5 10 C2
Jan Palach Av. CW5 10 C5
John Gresty Dri. CW5 11 G2
Jubilee Gdns. CW5 10 C5
Jubilee Ter. CW5 10 C4
Kensington Dri. CW5 11 G4
*King Pl, Beam St. CW5 10 C3
Kingfisher Clo. CW5 10 C1
Kings Ct. CW5 10 A3
Kings La. CW5 10 A3
Laburnam Av. CW5 10 C4
Lady Helen Walk. CW5 10 C3
Lakeside View. CW5 10 B6
Larkspur Clo. CW5 10 C1
Lea Dri. CW5 10 A4
Lewis Clo. CW5 11 E4
Lomax Rd. CW5 11 G3
London Rd. CW5 10 C4
Love La. CW5 10 A3
Mainwaring Clo. CW5 11 E5
Maisterson Ct. CW5 10 C3
Malbank. CW5 10 B3
Manor Rd. CW5 10 B2
Manor Rd North. CW5 10 B1
Mansion Ct. CW5 10 C4
Mark St. CW5 11 H2
Market St. CW5 10 C3
Marlowe Dri. CW5 10 C5
Marsh La. CW5 10 A5
Mayflower Rd. CW5 10 C1
Meadowvale Clo. CW5 10 C1
Meeanee Dri. CW5 10 A4
Mercer Way. CW5 10 C1
Middlewich Rd. CW5 10 C2
Mill St. CW5 10 B3
Mill Way. CW5 10 D6
Millfields. CW5 10 A4
Millstone La. CW5 10 C3
Monks La. CW5 10 C3
Monks Orchard. CW5 10 C3
Moorfields. CW5 11 H3
Mount Clo. CW5 10 D3
Mount Dri. CW5 10 D3
Murrayfield Dri. CW5 11 G3
Nantwich By-Pass. CW5 10 B1
Newbold Way. CW5 10 B5
Newcastle Rd. CW5 11 E4
Newland Way. CW5 11 E5
Nixons Row. CW5 10 A3
North Crofts. CW5 10 A3
*Nuthurst Gdns,
  Mansion Ct. CW5 10 C4
Oak Bank Clo. CW5 11 H4
Oak Gro. CW5 10 C6
Oatmarket. CW5 10 B3
Orchard Cres. CW5 10 C6
Orchard St. CW5 11 H3
Pall Mall. CW5 10 C4
Park Mills Clo. CW5 11 H3
Park Rd, Nantwich. CW5 10 B5
Park Rd, Willaston. CW5 11 F3
Park Vw. CW5 10 C5
Parkfield Dri. CW5 10 C5
Pear Tree Field. CW5 10 D5
Penlington Ct. CW5 10 D3
Pepper St. CW5 10 B3
Pillory St. CW5 10 B4
Pine Walk. CW5 10 C5
Pollard Dri. CW5 11 E4
Potter Clo. CW5 11 G4
Pratchitts Row. CW5 10 C4
Prince Edward St. CW5 10 B2
Princess Way. CW5 10 D3
*Queen St,
  Pillory St. CW5 10 B4
Queens Dri. CW5 10 B3
Ray Av. CW5 10 C1
Rectory Clo. CW5 10 C3
Red Lion La. CW5 10 B3
Regents Gate. CW5 10 D4
Rigsbys Row. CW5 10 C3

Riverbank Clo. CW5 10 C1
Riverside. CW5 10 B4
Rookery Clo. CW5 10 C5
Rookery Dri. CW5 10 C5
St Albans Dri. CW5 10 C5
St Annes La. CW5 10 B3
St Josephs Way. CW5 10 D4
St Lawrence Ct. CW5 10 C3
St Marys Rd. CW5 10 B2
St Nicholas Ct. CW5 10 C4
Saltmeadows. CW5 10 A3
Sandford Rd. CW5 10 C2
Scaife Rd. CW5 10 C3
School La. CW5 10 C3
Second Wood St. CW5 10 B3
Shannon Clo. CW5 11 G3
Shrewbridge Cres. CW5 10 B4
Shrewbridge Rd. CW5 10 B4
South Crofts. CW5 10 C3
Spring Gdns. CW5 10 C4
Stapeley Ter. CW5 10 D4
Station Rd. CW5 10 C4
Station Vw. CW5 10 C4
Stonebridge Rd. CW5 10 B6
Swine Mkt. CW5 10 B3
Sycamore Clo. CW5 10 D1
Tanners Way. CW5 10 B5
Tenchersfield. CW5 10 C4
The Beeches. CW5 10 C4
The Blankney. CW5 10 B4
The Broadway. CW5 10 D3
The Crescent. CW5 10 C3
The Fields. CW5 11 G4
The Gullet. CW5 10 C3
The Paddock. CW5 11 G4
The Pike. CW5 10 C6
The Spinney. CW5 11 G2
Tinkersfield. CW5 11 E5
Tricketts La. CW5 11 H3
Tricketts Mews. CW5 11 H3
Tudor Way. CW5 10 B6
Turner St. CW5 10 C3
Vauxhall Pl. CW5 10 C1
Vauxhall Rd. CW5 10 B1
Victoria Mill Dri. CW5 11 G3
Volunteer Av. CW5 10 C3
Volunteer Fields. CW5 10 C3
Wall Fields Clo. CW5 10 B2
Wall Fields Rd. CW5 10 B2
Wall La. CW5 10 B3
Water Lode. CW5 10 B3
Weaver Bank. CW5 10 B3
Weaver Rd. CW5 10 C2
Weaverside. CW5 10 C6
Wellington Rd. CW5 10 C4
Welsh Row. CW5 10 A3
Welshmens La. CW5 10 A2
Wesley Clo. CW5 10 C3
Western Av. CW5 10 C6
Whitehall Ct. CW5 10 B3
Whitehouse La. CW5 10 D1
Whitewell Clo. CW5 10 D3
Whitlow Av. CW5 10 C5
Wickstead Clo. CW5 11 E4
Willaston Hall Gdns. CW5 11 G3
Willow Clo. CW5 10 D2
Windsor Av. CW5 10 C5
Wistaston Rd. CW5 11 H3
Woodland Av. CW5 10 D3
Worthington Clo. CW5 11 E4
Wybunbury La. CW5 11 E5
Wybunbury Rd. CW5 11 H4
Wyche Av. CW5 10 A3
Wyche Ho Bank. CW5 10 B3
Yew Tree Dri. CW5 10 A3

SANDBACH

Abbey Rd. CW11 4 B3
Acacia Dri. CW11 4 B2
Adlington Dri. CW11 5 F2
Alderley Clo. CW11 5 F2
Angelina Clo. CW11 4 A2
Anvil Clo. CW11 4 C6
Arley Walk. CW11 4 A4

Name	Ref	Name	Ref
Armitstead Rd. CW11	4 C5	Dingle Bank. CW11	5 E3
Austen Clo. CW11	4 A3	Dingle La. CW11	5 E3
Bagmere Clo. CW11	4 C2	Doddington Dri. CW11	5 F1
Bailey Cres. CW11	5 G3	Dorfold Clo. CW11	5 F2
Barlow Way. CW11	4 D1	Dove Clo. CW11	5 D1
Bath St. CW11	5 E3	Drovers Way. CW11	4 D4
Beech Gro. CW11	5 F3	Dukes Cres. CW11	4 D1
Belle Vue Ter. CW11	4 D3	Dunham Clo. CW11	5 F3
Belmont Av. CW11	4 D2	Eaton Clo. CW11	5 E2
Betchton Clo. CW11	5 F2	Elanor Rd. CW11	4 A2
Betchton Rd. CW11	5 F6	Elizabeth Clo. CW11	4 A2
Birch Gdns. CW11	5 E3	Ellesmere Clo. CW11	4 C1
Birtles Clo. CW11	5 E2	Elm Tree La. CW11	4 A1
Blackacres Clo. CW11	4 C3	Elton Crossings Rd. CW11	4 A3
Blakemere Way. CW11	4 C1	Elton Rd. CW11	4 A4
Bold St. CW11	5 E3	Elworth Rd. CW11	4 A3
Bollin Clo. CW11	4 B2	Elworth St. CW11	4 D2
Booth Av. CW11	5 F3	Etherow Clo. CW11	4 B2
Boothsmere Clo. CW11	4 C1	Ettiley Av. CW11	4 A4
Boulton Clo. CW11	5 F6	Eva St. CW11	4 B1
Bowles Clo. CW11	4 C3	Fairfield Av. CW11	4 D4
Bradwall Rd. CW11	5 E2	Ferndale Clo. CW11	5 F4
Bradwall St. CW11	4 D2	Fields Dri. CW11	4 D4
Bramall Clo. CW11	5 E2	First Av. CW11	4 D4
Brereton Clo. CW11	5 F2	Flat La. CW11	5 E3
Bridgemere Clo. CW11	4 C1	Forge Fields. CW11	4 C6
Brindley Park. CW11	4 C6	Foundry La. CW11	4 A2
Brock Hollow. CW11	4 B5	Front St. CW11	5 E3
Brook Ct. CW11	5 E3	Game St. CW11	4 C6
Brook Ter. CW11	4 C6	Gawsworth Dri. CW11	5 F2
Brookhouse Rd. CW11	5 E3	George St. CW11	4 B1
Brookland Dri. CW11	5 G3	Georges Walk. CW11	5 E3
Brookmere Clo. CW11	4 B1	Gibson Cres. CW11	4 A3
Browning Clo. CW11	4 A4	Goldsmith Dri. CW11	4 A3
Budworth Clo. CW11	4 B2	Gowy Clo. CW11	4 B1
Byron Clo. CW11	4 A3	Grange Clo. CW11	4 C2
Capesthorne Clo. CW11	5 F2	Grange Way. CW11	4 C2
Cecil Rigby Clo. CW11	5 E3	Green Acres. CW11	4 D2
Cestria Clo. CW11	4 A2	Green St. CW11	5 E2
Chapel St, Sandbach. CW11	4 D3	Hartford Clo. CW11	5 F2
Chapel St, Wheelock. CW11	4 D6	Hassall La. CW11	5 F6
Chapelmere Clo. CW11	4 B2	Hatchmere La. CW11	4 C2
Charlesworth Ct. CW11	5 F3	Hawk St. CW11	5 E3
Chartwell Park. CW11	4 D5	Hawthorn Dri. CW11	5 F3
Chesterton Gro. CW11	4 A3	Heath Av. CW11	5 G3
Church La. CW11	5 H1	Heath Clo. CW11	5 G3
Church St. CW11	5 E3	Heath Rd. CW11	5 F3
Clifton Rd. CW11	4 A2	Henshall Dri. CW11	5 F1
Coldmoss Dri. CW11	5 F5	High St. CW11	5 E3
Coleridge Clo. CW11	4 A4	Hightown. CW11	5 E3
Colley La. CW11	5 F4	Hill St. CW11	4 A2
Commons Mill. CW11	5 E2	Hind Heath La. CW11	4 C5
Condliffe Clo. CW11	5 E4	Hind Heath Rd. CW11	4 B4
Congleton Rd. CW11	5 E3	Holland Clo. CW11	5 E4
Cookesmere La. CW11	4 C1	Holly Heath Clo. CW11	5 F4
Coopers Opening. CW11	4 D2	Hope St. CW11	5 E3
Coronation Cres. CW11	4 D4	Houndings La. CW11	4 D5
Cottons La. CW11	4 D6	Hungerford Pl. CW11	4 D4
Coverdale Fold. CW11	4 A4	**INDUSTRIAL & RETAIL:**	
Crabmill Dri. CW11	4 B2	Lodge Rd Ind Est. CW11	4 B4
Crewe Rd. CW11	4 C5	Moss La	
Cross La. CW11	5 F4	Business Centre. CW11	4 A3
Cross St. CW11	5 E2	Springvale	
Crown Bank. CW11	5 E3	Business Centre. CW11	4 A3
Cumbermere Dri. CW11	4 B2	Zan Industrial Pk. CW11	4 D6
Daisybank Dri. CW11	5 F3	King St. CW11	4 B1
Dalton Ct. CW11	4 B2	Langley Clo. CW11	5 F1
Dane Clo. CW11	4 B2	Latham Rd. CW11	4 D4
Davenport Clo. CW11	5 F1	Laurel Clo. CW11	5 E4
Dean Clo. CW11	4 B1	Lawrence Clo. CW11	4 A3
Deans La. CW11	4 B3	Lawton Way. CW11	4 B1
Dee Clo. CW11	4 B1	Lea Clo. CW11	5 F4
Delamere Clo. CW11	4 C1	Lightley Clo. CW11	4 D5
Dickens Clo. CW11	4 A3	Lightley Ct. CW11	4 D5

Name	Ref	Name	Ref
Lime Clo. CW11	4 D2	Rostherne Way. CW11	4 C2
Linden Ct. CW11	4 C6	Rowan Clo. CW11	4 C2
Lodge Rd. CW11	4 B4	Ruscoe Av. CW11	4 B3
London Rd. CW11	4 A1	St Johns Way. CW11	5 G3
Manifold Clo. CW11	4 B1	St Peters Rise. CW11	4 B2
Manor Rd. CW11	5 F3	St Stephens Ct. CW11	4 B2
Manor Way. CW11	5 G3	Salt Line Way. CW11	4 A2
Maple Clo. CW11	5 F3	Sanbec Way. CW11	5 E3
Market Sq. CW11	5 E3	Sandy La. CW11	4 A4
Marlowe Clo. CW11	4 A4	Saxon Way. CW11	5 E3
Marriott Rd. CW11	4 C6	School La, Elworth. CW11	4 B2
Marsh Green Rd. CW11	4 A1	School La,	
Masefield Way. CW11	4 A4	Sandbach Heath. CW11	5 H3
Meadow Gate Clo. CW11	4 A4	Scott Clo. CW11	4 A3
Middlewich Rd. CW11	4 B2	Second Av. CW11	4 D4
Millbuck Way. CW11	4 A3	Shelley Ct. CW11	4 A3
Mill Hill Dri. CW11	4 D4	Silver Ter. CW11	5 G3
Mill Hill La. CW11	4 D4	Skeath Clo. CW11	5 G3
Mill La. CW11	4 D6	Smithfield La. CW11	5 F3
Mill Row. CW11	5 F3	Smithy Walk. CW11	4 C6
Milton Way. CW11	4 A3	Somerford Clo. CW11	5 F1
Moreton Clo. CW11	5 E2	Southey Clo. CW11	4 A3
Mornington Clo. CW11	4 B2	Stannerhouse La. CW11	5 G6
Mortimer Dri. CW11	5 F4	Station Rd. CW11	4 A1
Moss La. CW11	4 A2	Station Vw. CW11	4 A1
Moston Rd. CW11	4 A4	Sterne Clo. CW11	4 A3
Mulberry Gdns. CW11	4 A2	Stringer Av. CW11	5 F3
New St. CW11	4 A2	Swallow Clo. CW11	4 D1
Newall Av. CW11	4 D3	Sweet Tooth La. CW11	4 D2
Newfield St. CW11	5 E2	Swettenham Clo. CW11	5 F2
Newcastle La. CW11	5 H5	Sycamore Gro. CW11	4 D1
Norton Way. CW11	4 A2	Tabley Clo. CW11	4 B2
Oak St. CW11	4 A1	Tame Clo. CW11	4 B1
Oakley Clo. CW11	4 D1	Tatton Dri. CW11	5 E2
Oakmere Clo. CW11	4 C2	Tatton Clo. CW11	4 C2
Oakwood Cres. CW11	5 G3	Telford Gdns. CW11	4 C6
Offley Av. CW11	5 E2	Thackery Ct. CW11	4 A3
Offley Rd. CW11	5 E2	The Avenue. CW11	4 B1
Old Mill Rd. CW11	5 E3	The Commons. CW11	5 E3
Oldfield Rd. CW11	4 C5	The Coppice. CW11	4 B2
Ordsall Clo. CW11	4 C6	*The Gardens,	
Ormerod Clo. CW11	5 E4	Old Mill Rd. CW11	5 E3
Osborne Clo. CW11	4 A4	The Hill. CW11	5 F3
Ossmere Clo. CW11	4 C1	The Spinney. CW11	5 F3
Palmer Rd. CW11	5 E4	The Willows. CW11	5 E2
Park House Dri. CW11	5 F1	The Woodlands. CW11	5 F4
Park La. CW11	4 C3	Third Av. CW11	4 D4
Pear Tree Clo. CW11	5 G3	Thornbrook Way. CW11	4 A4
Peckforton Clo. CW11	4 B1	Tiverton Clo. CW11	5 F2
Penda Way. CW11	5 E3	Town Fields. CW11	4 D4
Pickmere Clo. CW11	4 C2	Twemlow Av. CW11	5 E2
Pickwick Clo. CW11	5 F1	Union St. CW11	4 D3
Pine Gro. CW11	5 F3	Vicarage Gdns. CW11	4 B1
Plant St. CW11	4 D2	Vicarage La, Elworth. CW11	4 B2
Platt Av. CW11	4 D2	Vicarage La,	
Price Av. CW11	4 D4	Sandbach. CW11	5 G5
Price Dri. CW11	4 D4	Victoria St. CW11	4 D2
Princess Dri. CW11	4 C1	Waterside Mews. CW11	4 C6
Proctors Rd. CW11	4 A4	Weaver Clo. CW11	4 B2
Queens Dri. CW11	4 D1	Well Bank. CW11	5 E3
Radbroke Clo. CW11	5 F1	Welles St. CW11	5 E2
Radcliffe Rd. CW11	4 C6	Wesley Av. CW11	5 E3
Radnor Clo. CW11	4 B2	West Way. CW11	4 C5
Randle Bennett Clo. CW11	4 B2	Wheelock Wharf. CW11	4 D6
Raven Clo. CW11	4 D1	Willow Dri. CW11	5 G2
Ravenscroft Clo. CW11	5 F2	Withington Clo. CW11	5 F2
Redesmere Clo. CW11	4 C2	Woodside Dri. CW11	5 F3
Reynolds La. CW11	5 H2	Wordsworth Clo. CW11	4 A3
Richardson Clo. CW11	4 A3	Wrenmere Clo. CW11	4 B1
Richmond Clo. CW11	4 B2	Wrights La. CW11	5 G3
Riley Clo. CW11	4 B4	Zan Dri. CW11	4 C6
Robin Clo. CW11	4 D1		
Roman Way. CW11	4 B2		
Rookery Clo. CW11	4 A4		

ESTATE PUBLICATIONS

RED BOOKS

ALDERSHOT, CAMBERLEY
ALFRETON, BELPER, RIPLEY
ASHFORD, TENTERDEN
AYLESBURY, TRING
BANGOR, CAERNARFON
BARNSTAPLE, ILFRACOMBE
BASILDON, BILLERICAY
BASINGSTOKE, ANDOVER
BATH, BRADFORD-ON-AVON
BEDFORD
BIRMINGHAM, WOLVERHAMPTON, COVENTRY
BODMIN, WADEBRIDGE
BOURNEMOUTH, POOLE, CHRISTCHURCH
BRACKNELL
BRENTWOOD
BRIGHTON, LEWES, NEWHAVEN, SEAFORD
BRISTOL
BROMLEY (London Bromley)
BURTON-UPON-TRENT, SWADLINCOTE
BURY ST. EDMUNDS
CAMBRIDGE
CARDIFF
CARLISLE
CHELMSFORD, BRAINTREE, MALDON, WITHAM
CHESTER
CHESTERFIELD
CHICHESTER, BOGNOR REGIS
COLCHESTER, CLACTON
CORBY, KETTERING
COVENTRY
CRAWLEY & MID SUSSEX
CREWE
DERBY, HEANOR, CASTLE DONINGTON
EASTBOURNE, BEXHILL, SEAFORD, NEWHAVEN
EDINBURGH, MUSSELBURGH, PENICUIK
EXETER, EXMOUTH
FALKIRK, GRANGEMOUTH
FAREHAM, GOSPORT
FLINTSHIRE TOWNS
FOLKESTONE, DOVER, DEAL & ROMNEY MARSH
GLASGOW, & PAISLEY
GLOUCESTER, CHELTENHAM
GRAVESEND, DARTFORD
GRAYS, THURROCK
GREAT YARMOUTH, LOWESTOFT
GRIMSBY, CLEETHORPES
GUILDFORD, WOKING
HARLOW, BISHOPS STORTFORD
HARROGATE, KNARESBOROUGH
HASTINGS, BEXHILL, RYE
HEREFORD
HERTFORD, HODDESDON, WARE
HIGH WYCOMBE
HUNTINGDON, ST. NEOTS
IPSWICH, FELIXSTOWE
ISLE OF MAN
ISLE OF WIGHT TOWNS
KENDAL
KIDDERMINSTER
KINGSTON-UPON-HULL
LANCASTER, MORECAMBE
LEICESTER, LOUGHBOROUGH
LINCOLN
LLANDUDNO, COLWYN BAY
LUTON, DUNSTABLE
MACCLESFIELD
MAIDSTONE
MANSFIELD, MANSFIELD WOODHOUSE
MEDWAY, GILLINGHAM
MILTON KEYNES
NEW FOREST TOWNS
NEWBURY, THATCHAM
NEWPORT, CHEPSTOW
NEWQUAY
NEWTOWN, WELSHPOOL
NORTHAMPTON
NORTHWICH, WINSFORD
NORWICH
NOTTINGHAM, EASTWOOD, HUCKNALL, ILKESTON
NUNEATON, BEDWORTH
OXFORD, ABINGDON
PENZANCE, ST. IVES
PETERBOROUGH
PLYMOUTH, IVYBRIDGE, SALTASH, TORPOINT
PORTSMOUTH, HAVANT, WATERLOOVILLE
READING
REDDITCH, BROMSGROVE

REIGATE, BANSTEAD, LEATHERHEAD, DORKING
RHYL, PRESTATYN
RUGBY
ST. ALBANS, WELWYN, HATFIELD
ST. AUSTELL
SALISBURY, AMESBURY, WILTON
SCUNTHORPE
SEVENOAKS
SHREWSBURY
SITTINGBOURNE, FAVERSHAM, ISLE OF SHEPPEY
SLOUGH, MAIDENHEAD, WINDSOR
SOUTHAMPTON, EASTLEIGH
SOUTHEND-ON-SEA
STAFFORD
STEVENAGE, HITCHIN, LETCHWORTH
STIRLING
STOKE-ON-TRENT
STROUD, NAILSWORTH
SWANSEA, NEATH, PORT TALBOT
SWINDON, CHIPPENHAM, MARLBOROUGH
TAUNTON, BRIDGWATER
TELFORD
THANET, CANTERBURY, HERNE BAY, WHITSTABLE
TORBAY (Torquay, Paignton, Newton Abbot)
TRURO, FALMOUTH
TUNBRIDGE WELLS, TONBRIDGE, CROWBOROUGH
WARWICK, ROYAL LEAMINGTON SPA &
   STRATFORD UPON AVON
WATFORD, HEMEL HEMPSTEAD
WELLINGBOROUGH
WESTON-SUPER-MARE, CLEVEDON
WEYMOUTH, DORCHESTER
WINCHESTER, NEW ARLESFORD
WORCESTER, DROITWICH
WORTHING, LITTLEHAMPTON, ARUNDEL
WREXHAM
YORK

COUNTY RED BOOKS (Town Centre Maps)

BEDFORDSHIRE
BERKSHIRE
BUCKINGHAMSHIRE
CAMBRIDGESHIRE
CHESHIRE
CORNWALL
DERBYSHIRE
DEVON
DORSET
ESSEX
GLOUCESTERSHIRE
HAMPSHIRE
HEREFORDSHIRE
HERTFORDSHIRE
KENT
LEICESTERSHIRE & RUTLAND
LINCOLNSHIRE
NORFOLK
NORTHAMPTONSHIRE
NOTTINGHAMSHIRE
OXFORDSHIRE
SHROPSHIRE
SOMERSET
STAFFORDSHIRE
SUFFOLK
SURREY
SUSSEX (EAST)
SUSSEX (WEST)
WILTSHIRE
WORCESTERSHIRE

OTHER MAPS

KENT TO CORNWALL (1:460,000)
CHINA (1:6,000,000)
INDIA (1:3,750,000)
INDONESIA (1:4,000,000)
NEPAL (1,800,000)
SOUTH EAST ASIA (1:6,000,000)
THAILAND (1:1,600,000)

STREET PLANS

CARDIFF
EDINBURGH TOURIST PLAN
ST. ALBANS
WOLVERHAMPTON

OFFICIAL TOURIST & LEISURE MAPS

SOUTH EAST ENGLAND (1:200,000)
KENT & EAST SUSSEX (1:150,000)
SUSSEX & SURREY (1:150,000)
SUSSEX (1:50,000)
SOUTHERN ENGLAND (1:200,000)
ISLE OF WIGHT (1:50,000)
WESSEX (1:200,000)
DORSET (1:50,000)
DEVON & CORNWALL (1:200,000)
CORNWALL (1:180,000)
DEVON (1:200,000)
DARTMOOR & SOUTH DEVON COAST (1:100,000)
EXMOOR & NORTH DEVON COAST (1:100,000)
GREATER LONDON M25 (1:80,000)
EAST ANGLIA (1:200,000)
CHILTERNS & THAMES VALLEY (1:200,000)
THE COTSWOLDS (1:110,000)
COTSWOLDS & SEVERN VALLEY (1:200,000)
WALES (1:250,000)
THE SHIRES OF MIDDLE ENGLAND (1:250,000)
THE MID SHIRES (Staffs, Shrops, etc.) (1:200,000)
PEAK DISTRICT (1:100,000)
SNOWDONIA (1:125,000)
YORKSHIRE (1:200,000)
YORKSHIRE DALES (1:125,000)
NORTH YORKSHIRE MOORS (1:125,000)
NORTH WEST ENGLAND (1:200,000)
ISLE OF MAN (1:60,000)
NORTH PENNINES & LAKES (1:200,000)
LAKE DISTRICT (1:75,000)
BORDERS OF ENGLAND & SCOTLAND (1:200,000)
BURNS COUNTRY (1:200,000)
HEART OF SCOTLAND (1:200,000)
GREATER GLASGOW (1:150,000)
EDINBURGH & THE LOTHIANS (1:150,000)
ISLE OF ARRAN (1:63,360)
FIFE (1:100,000)
LOCH LOMOND & TROSSACHS (1:150,000)
ARGYLL THE ISLES & LOCH LOMOND (1:275,000)
PERTHSHIRE, DUNDEE & ANGUS (1:150,000)
FORT WILLIAM, BEN NEVIS, GLEN COE (1:185,000)
IONA (1:10,000) & MULL (1:115,000)
GRAMPIAN HIGHLANDS (1:185,000)
LOCH NESS & INVERNESS (1:150,000)
SKYE & LOCHALSH (1:130,000)
ARGYLL & THE ISLES (1:200,000)
CAITHNESS & SUTHERLAND (1:185,000)
HIGHLANDS OF SCOTLAND (1:275,000)
WESTERN ISLES (1:125,000)
ORKNEY & SHETLAND (1:128,000)
ENGLAND & WALES (1:650,000)
SCOTLAND (1:500,000)
HISTORIC SCOTLAND (1:500,000)
SCOTLAND CLAN MAP (1:625,000)
BRITISH ISLES (1:1,100,000)
GREAT BRITAIN (1:1,100,000)

EUROPEAN LEISURE MAPS

EUROPE (1:3,100,000)
BENELUX (1:600,000)
FRANCE (1:1,000,000)
GERMANY (1:1,000,000)
IRELAND (1:625,000)
ITALY (1:1,000,000)
SPAIN & PORTUGAL (1,1,000,000)
CROSS CHANNEL VISITORS' MAP (1:530,000)
WORLD (1:35,000,000)
WORLD FLAT

TOWNS IN NORTHERN FRANCE STREET ATLAS
BOULOGNE SHOPPERS MAP
CALAIS SHOPPERS MAP
DIEPPE SHOPPERS MAP

ESTATE PUBLICATIONS are also
Distributors in the UK for:

INTERNATIONAL TRAVEL MAPS, Canada
HALLWAG, Switzerland
ORDNANCE SURVEY

Catalogue and prices from:
ESTATE PUBLICATIONS
Bridewell House, Tenterden, Kent. TN30 6EP.
Tel: 01580 764225   Fax: 01580 763720
www.estate-publications.co.uk